Ba
Carpentry
Projects

JOHN BOWLER

MINI · WORKBOOK · SERIES

MEREHURST

CONTENTS

A handrail and balustrade (top), architraves and skirting boards (far left) and a damaged timber floor (left)

Hanging a picture

Hanging a picture or mirror neatly on a wall is a common household task. It should be securely fixed so that it won't fall and so that the wall suffers minimal damage.

MATERIALS AND TOOLS

- Appropriate fitting
- Hammer
- Punch
- Power drill
- Screwdriver

DECIDING ON HARDWARE

For a picture to be hung safely, you must ensure that the fitting you choose can support the weight of the picture and that it is suitable for the type of wall. It is more often the wall that fails than the fitting.

SOLID MASONRY WALLS

The most common fittings for solid walls are screw-in or drive-in types.

- Wall plugs are made from plastic and expand when the screw is driven in. For most pictures a small diameter plug of 5 or 6 mm will be sufficient. Wall plugs are available up to 50 mm long and can be purchased in packets or as a continuous length. Wall plugs are not recommended for use in plaster or lime mortar joints.
- Drive pins are inserted into a drilled hole and the pin hammered in through a metal hook.
- Drive-in pin types may be used for lightweight pictures. To insert them,

hold the pin between your thumb and forefinger with the back of the hook parallel to the wall. Hammer the pin into the wall as if you were hammering in a nail, until the hook sits against the wall.
- There are also a number of patented drive-in hooks available.

HOLLOW WALLS

A picture can be fixed to a hollow wall by solid fixings into a stud or by plasterboard wall plugs or anchors. These give you more freedom when deciding where to hang your picture. They will carry most pictures but for large, heavy pictures it is better to use a solid fixing.

There are a number of patented plasterboard wall plugs available.
- Spring or gravity toggles. These are used with a picture hook. Place a washer over the face of the wall to cover the hole and prevent the screw head pulling through.
- Hook toggles can be used although they stick out from the wall a little more than the hooked washer does.
- Metal hollow anchors concertina up when the screw is tightened and have excellent holding power.
- Plastic butterfly-type toggles are also available.

The type of fitting used to hang a picture or mirror on a wall depends on the type of wall, whether it is solid or framed, and whether a stud is located in the required spot.

• Plasterboard screw wall plugs fit on the end of a screwdriver and pierce the wall lining as they are screwed in. Only light pressure is needed as the plug drills its own hole. A screw or hook is then inserted.

SURFACE FITTINGS
Double-sided tape hooks are suitable for lightweight application and are only as good as the base they are attached to. If the paint is not sound, then the hook will lift off the wall.

The picture rails and hooks still used in some older homes will carry a large painting with ease.

USING A WALL PLUG (MASONRY WALLS)

1 Mark the wall with a centre punch. The indentation will prevent the drill from wandering.

2 Place the correct size of masonry bit in a power drill (a hammer–action type if you have one). The bit size should match the plug size. Select a slow speed and position the drill against the wall so that the bit rests in the indentation.

3 Drill the hole 25 mm deep, at first using just enough pressure to stop the drill wandering. When the drill starts to create a hole, apply more

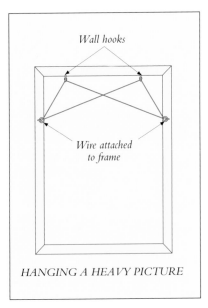

Wall hooks

Wire attached to frame

HANGING A HEAVY PICTURE

HINT

Masonry walls in older houses may be unstable so take care when drilling into them.

pressure so that the bit doesn't wander. Drill the hole at 90 degrees to the face of the wall, moving the bit in and out slightly as you go to clear out the waste. Test the depth of the hole by pushing a nail or screw to the bottom and match it with the plug. (If you are drilling into a plaster rendered wall, the plug should finish below the plaster.)

4 Tap the plug into the hole the required depth. If you are using a continuous plug, push it into the bottom of the hole, then pull it back out 3 mm and cut it off with a chisel.

5 Use the correct gauge screw for the plug, for example, a 5 mm plug needs a 4 or 6 gauge screw. Place the screw through the picture hook, align the point of the screw with the centre of the plug and screw it in firmly. Be careful not to overtighten the screw.

USING A SOLID FIXING (HOLLOW WALLS)

1 Locate a wall stud by using a stud finder or tap the wall and listen for a solid sound. Another way is to look across the wall at an angle with the light reflecting on the face of the wall to see any blemishes made by the plasterboard fixings.

2 Draw a vertical line up or down the correct height.

3 Drill a hole the appropriate size for your screw through the lining and into the stud.

4 Screw through a picture hook into the hole. (For a steel-framed wall, use a self-tapping screw.)

HOLLOW WALL PLUGS

1 Locate the position for the fixing and then drill a hole the size recommended by the manufacturer.

2 Collapse the plug and push it through the hole. Once it is through the lining it will expand against the back of the lining.

3 Place a picture hook over the plug and screw through it into the plug until it fits tightly.

HOLLOW WALLS

If there is not a wall stud in the appropriate place, timber can sometimes be fitted into the wall cavity via the eaves space, but take care not to damage the plasterboard in the ceiling or wall.

Alternatively, place a hook in a stud that will be covered by the picture with a hollow wall plug to one side. This will pull the picture over to that side while the main weight of the picture is supported by the solid fixing.

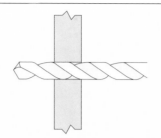

1 Drill the hole.

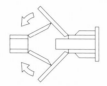

2 Squeeze the wings together.

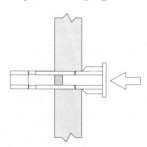

3 Insert the anchor.

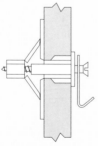

4 Screw through the picture hook.

HOLLOW WALL ANCHOR

Hanging a door

Hanging a door and fitting the locks and handle are basic carpentry projects that can be undertaken with a minimum of experience and tools.

MATERIALS AND TOOLS

- Door
- Two hinges and screws
- Lock/latch set
- Tape and pencil
- Hand plane
- Chisel: 25 mm
- Marking gauge
- Electric drill
- Powerbore or spade bit
- Screwdriver

TYPES OF DOORS

There are two types of doors: solid doors and hollow doors, which have a timber frame with a plywood, MDF or hardboard sheet on each side. Either can be flush or panelled. Most modern doors are hollow.

A standard door can be 2000, 2030 or 2170 mm high, and 520, 620, 720, 770, 820 or 870 mm wide. It is usually 35 or 40 mm thick. If the opening is not standard, you may need a 'special' door. It can be made to fit but will be expensive. A standard door can usually be trimmed to size. Some have an edge strip on the sides. If you need to replace it, use matching timber, sanded flush with the door.

FITTING THE DOOR

1 A door requires clearance of 3 mm on each side and the top, with a slightly larger clearance on the bottom, usually 5 mm above a floor covering or 10–25 mm above the floor. For example, if the height from the floor to the top rebate is 2040 mm, the door height will be about 2025 mm, and if the width from rebate to rebate is 725 mm, the door width will be 719 mm. In this case a standard door measuring 2030 x 720 mm could be used.

2 Determine the lock side of the door. Hollow doors are constructed with an extra block inside the door to fit the lock through (the lock block). There may be a sticker on the side or you can tap the door and listen for the solid sound.

3 Set up the door in the opening with the lock side on the correct side. Wedge the door into one top corner of the frame, using a pair of timber wedges (or old chisel) placed under the bottom of the door. Check the fit. If the door fits evenly in the corner it will only need to be trimmed for clearance. You may need to plane the top and sides of the

The techniques of hanging a door are the same, no matter whether it is a single-leaf or double-leaf door. Here a standard door has been split to form a double door that needs only half the clearance to open.

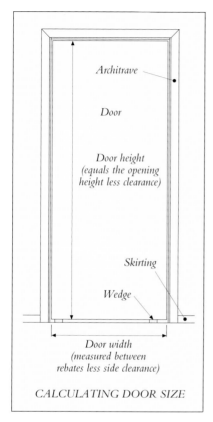

Architrave

Door

Door height
(equals the opening
height less clearance)

Skirting

Wedge

Door width
(measured between
rebates less side clearance)

CALCULATING DOOR SIZE

don't remove too much. Generally, an even amount of up to 10 mm is removed from each side of the door. Use a hand plane as you are less likely to remove too much and make the door too small. If you are taking off large amounts with a power saw or electric plane, stop at least 1 mm from the finished size and complete with a hand plane. To hold the door steady while planing, use a timber piece that has a recess cut in one edge the same thickness as the door. Use a small wedge to secure the job.

4 Once the door is fitted into the corner, hold it against the frame. Scribe down the fitting side with a pencil. Plane to this line. If necessary, repeat for an accurate fit.

5 Fit the top against the door head. With the door fitted into one top corner, plane the other edge to create an even gap of 4 mm down the side. Use an old chisel to lever the door up into position.

6 If desired, split the door (see the box on page 15).

door for an accurate fit. Hollow doors can be trimmed to fit the opening without affecting the strength of the door as long as you

3 When planing, hold the door steady in timber that has a recess cut in one edge the thickness of the door.

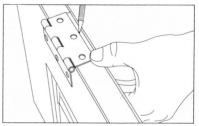

9 Open the hinge and use it to transfer the width of the leaf to the edge of the door.

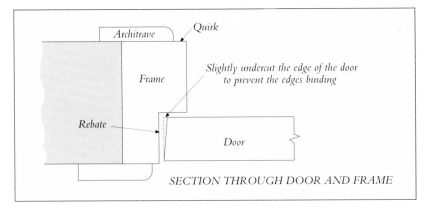

Quirk

Architrave

Frame

Slightly undercut the edge of the door to prevent the edges binding

Rebate

Door

SECTION THROUGH DOOR AND FRAME

HANGING THE DOOR

7 Slightly plane both long edges out of square (1 mm) to prevent the back binding when the door is opened and closed (see the diagram above).

8 Mark the hinge position on the door 175 mm down from the top and 225 mm up from the bottom. (Do, however, check the other doors in your house and mark out the new doors to match.) Mark the length of the hinge from this point and square lines across the edge of the door.

9 Set a marking gauge to the width of the hinge leaf and transfer it to the edge of the door, or use one leaf of the hinge on the edge.

10 Square the lines for the length 5 mm onto the face of the door.

11 Replace the door in the opening with a small coin on top and a wedge below. Transfer the hinge positions to the frame and square the lines across the frame face. Mark the width of the leaf. Place an 'X' on the face of the recess, so as not to cut on the wrong side of the line.

12 The hinge should fit neatly into the recesses that are cut into the edge

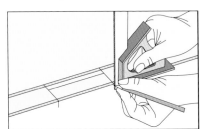

10 Square the lines indicating the length of the hinge 5 mm onto the face of the door.

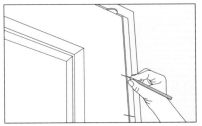

11 Wedge the door in the opening and use a pencil to transfer the hinge positions to the frame.

of the door and frame. Set the marking gauge and mark a line on the face of the doors and edge of the frame. Close the hinge. The gap between the leaves is the clearance required on the side of the door.

13 Cut the door recesses with a 25 mm chisel by lightly tapping the chisel with your hammer. Hold the chisel with the ground side down at an angle of 45 degrees. This raises the grain and makes removing waste easier. Chisel inside the set-out lines across the grain (not with it or you could accidentally split the door).

14 Pare away the waste to the required depth, guiding the chisel by hand. Do not use a hammer or push the chisel too hard or you may break out the back of the recess.

15 Once the recess is the correct depth, chisel out the rest to the set-out lines. Check the fit of the hinge. Adjust the recess as required. Check the distance from the edge of the recess to the back of the door. Then check the same distance on the

frame. The frame measurement should be 2 mm greater to prevent the door becoming hinge-bound. Adjust the set-out as required.

16 Cut the recess in the frame and check the hinge for fit. Remove all sharp edges on the doors with a hand plane or abrasive paper.

17 Place hinges in each recess on the door and drill the screw holes slightly off-centre towards the back of the hinge, so that the countersunk screws will pull the hinge tight into the back of the recess. Place the hinges in the frame recesses and drill one hole only (usually the centre one).

18 Fix the hinges to the door. The slots of slotted screws should run vertical. Stand the door at right angles to the frame and place the hinges in the recesses. Use a chisel or wedge to lift the door to align the hinges. Fix the hinges with one screw in each.

19 Test the swing of the door and, if correct, finish fixing the screws.

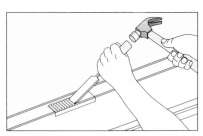

13 Cut the recess with a chisel held at a 45 degree angle, lightly tapping it with a hammer.

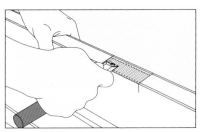

14 Pare away the waste to the required depth using a hand-held chisel. Don't push it too hard.

FITTING LOCKS/LATCHES

20 Read the instructions on the lock packaging. Determine the height of the latch (in hollow core doors find the timber lock block). Locks should be fixed at the same height as any others in the house.

21 Square a line across the edge and faces of the door for the centre of the latch. Fold the centring template around the door on the square line and tap a nail through it to mark the holes (see the diagram on page 14).

22 Place a powerbore or spade bit in an electric drill and bore the holes, moving it in and out to clear the waste. Drill the hole from one side until the point of the bit comes just through the other side of the door. Finish the hole from the other side.

23 Bore the hole in the edge for the tubular latch. Place the latch in this hole and trace around the faceplate. Mark the depth on the door edge. Hold the chisel at 45 degrees with the ground side down and cut the recess so the faceplate finishes flush.

24 Mark and drill the holes for the latch and handles. Fix with the screws supplied. If necessary, use a hacksaw to shorten the handle bar that goes through the door.

25 Push the door closed until the latch hits the frame and mark it with a pencil. Square these marks across the face of the frame.

DOOR PROBLEMS

Doors generally stick because they have not been fitted correctly or there has been movement in the building. In the latter case you should seek professional advice.

To fix a sticking door, you can remove it and plane the edges or sand off the layers of paint that have been applied over the years.

If you lay new floor coverings you may need to cut the bottom of the door. Measure the amount to be cut, then score and cut along the waste side of the line.

---

26 On the door edge, measure from the back face to the front of the latch. Mark a vertical line down the frame equal to this. Place the striking plate over the frame to line up with these lines. Trace around the inside of the plate to mark the recess for the lock. Chisel out the frame. Close the door, ensuring the lock lines up with the recess and is fully extended.

27 Place the striking plate over the recess, trace around it and cut in flush with your chisel. Screw the plate in place and check the operation of the latch. Adjust as required.

TO FINISH

28 Remove pencil or dirty marks with fine abrasive paper. Doors subjected to moisture (external, bathroom and laundry doors) should be sealed on all edges and faces.

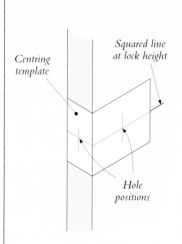

Centring template

Squared line at lock height

Hole positions

1 Fold centring template around the edge of the door and tap a nail through to mark hole positions.

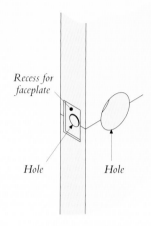

Recess for faceplate

Hole

Hole

2 Drill holes on centre marks, cut a recess in the edge to take faceplate and fit lock/latch and handles.

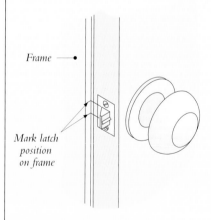

Frame

Mark latch position on frame

3 Locate latch position on frame and square lines across the face of the frame.

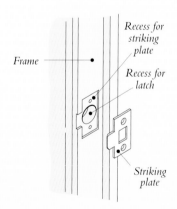

Frame

Recess for striking plate

Recess for latch

Striking plate

4 Place striking plate in position and mark latch recess. Cut it out. Trace and cut recess for striking plate. Screw in place.

FITTING A LOCK

SPLITTING A DOOR

1 Lay the door on trestles and mark the centre on the top and bottom edges. Square this mark across the edges. On the top face measure 6 mm towards the outside edge and square a line along the face and halfway down the edges. Turn the door over and repeat on the other side, measuring the other way from the centre line.

2 Cramp a straight edge to the door as a guide and set a circular saw at a depth equal to half the thickness of the door. Check the cutting notch lines up with the set-out and cut the door. Turn the door over and repeat.

3 While holding half of the door down, lift the other up. This splits the grain on the top and bottom rails, thus splitting the door.

4 Cut a 27 mm thick piece of timber for a lock block. Apply adhesive to both faces and insert it between the door panels.

5 Cut 27 mm thick timber to fit between the panels to form the fourth side of the frame. It should fit between the top and bottom rails. Glue it in place, keeping the outside edges flush. Leave to dry.

6 Lightly plane the edge so that the infill finishes flush.

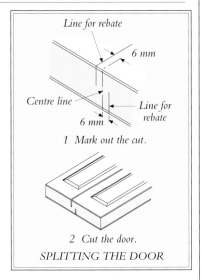

1 Mark out the cut.

2 Cut the door.

SPLITTING THE DOOR

7 Set up a router with an 18 mm straight bit and fence. Cut a rebate 13 mm wide and half the thickness of the door in depth, along the joining edges. Clean up the rebate with abrasive paper.

8 Place the two door halves together and check that the rebates line up. Adjust as required.

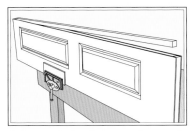

5 Insert timber between the panels and top and bottom rails to form the fourth side of the frame.

Carefully mitred architraves around doors and windows, and skirtings that fit neatly into corners provide elegant contrasting touches to a room as well as serving a useful purpose by covering the gaps around the wall cladding.

Replacing architraves and skirtings

Skirtings and architraves cover the gaps where the wall cladding meets the window or door frame, or the floor. They are available in a range of shapes and sizes.

MEASURING UP FOR ARCHITRAVES

1 Measure up for the lengths you will need, allowing for mitre joints and quirk (the edge of the frame left uncovered by the architrave). For an average doorway (2030 x 820 mm) you will need two pieces 2119 mm long and one piece 968 mm long. This is calculated as follows:

Door height (2030 mm) + clearance (18 mm) + quirk (5 mm) + width of top architrave (66 mm) = minimum length (2119 mm)

Width (820 mm) + clearance (6 mm) + quirk x 2 (10 mm) + width of side architraves x 2 (132 mm) = minimum width (968 mm)

As timber is often cut slightly over the stock sizes, you may be able to purchase two 2100 mm pieces for

MATERIALS AND TOOLS
● Architrave
● 50 x 2.75 mm lost-head nails
● PVA adhesive
● Filler
● Tape and pencil
● Chisel
● Hacksaw★
● Mitre box or mitre saw
● Tenon saw
● Hammer
● Hand plane★
★ In some situations only.

the side architraves (this is a stock size). However, measure the pieces before you take them home because if they are exactly 2100 mm long they will not be long enough. Timber suppliers carry a wide range of architraves and skirtings so that you can match existing ones. Take a sample piece with you when you go to the store.

REMOVING ARCHITRAVES

2 Drive a chisel into the joint between the frame and architrave. Do not chisel between the wall lining and architrave or you may

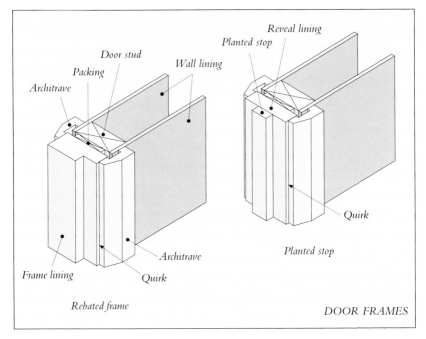

Reveal lining
Planted stop
Door stud
Packing
Wall lining
Architrave
Quirk
Architrave
Frame lining
Quirk
Planted stop
Rebated frame

DOOR FRAMES

damage the plaster. Once the joint is open sufficiently, place a scrap piece of timber between the chisel and the frame, to protect the timber.

3 Lever the architrave off carefully. If the chisel is damaging the surface too much or you want to re-use the architrave, open the joint just

enough to insert a hacksaw blade and cut through the nails. The architrave will then lift off easily.

4 Pull out or drive in any remaining nails. Sand the edge of the frame and fill as required. Repair any damage to the wall with plaster, and sand it to a smooth finish.

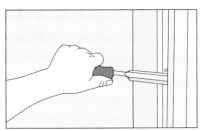

2 Drive a chisel into the joint between the frame and architrave, taking care not to damage the plaster.

3 Lever the architrave off carefully. If necessary, use a hacksaw blade to cut through the nails.

REPLACING ARCHITRAVES

5 Using a mitre saw, square one end of the new architrave. Stand the architrave in position over the frame so that it covers the gap between the frame and the wall.

6 Set the inside edge of the architrave back from the face of the frame 4–5 mm (for the quirk). Check the fit against the frame and wall. If the architrave does not sit flat against the wall, draw a pencil line down the outside edge of the architrave to show the amount to be removed. Plane the back face back to the line and check the fit again.

7 Repeat steps 5 and 6 on the other side of the doorway.

8 Mark the height of the doorway on the inside edge of each architrave, 4–5 mm higher than the frame. Place one architrave in a mitre box or mitre saw and cut the 45 degree angle. Repeat on the other piece. Check that you have one architrave for the left-hand side of the doorway and one for the right.

SCRIBING ARCHITRAVE INTO A CORNER

In some cases the architrave may need to be cut to fit into a corner. Fit it into the corner and tack it to the frame so it overlaps the inside edge and is parallel to the frame. Measure the amount of the overlap and add to this the required quirk. Cut a scrap of timber to this thickness. Holding a pencil against the block, run both down the wall to mark (scribe) a line down the architrave. Remove the architrave and plane it to shape. Reposition the architrave and fix it in place.

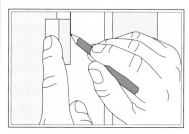

Place the scrap of timber against the wall and use a pencil to mark a line down the architrave.

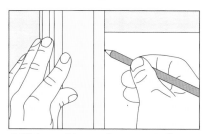

6 If the architrave does not sit flat on the wall, draw a line down the edge to show the amount to be removed.

8 Mark the height of the doorway on the inside face of the architrave, 4–5 mm higher than the frame.

TIMBER CONDITIONS

Timber is sold in three different conditions:

• sawn or rough sawn: sawn to a specific (nominal) size
• planed, either planed all round (PAR), planed on two sides (P2S) or double planed
• moulded: planed to a specific profile for architraves, window sills, skirting boards and so on

Planed timber is mostly sold using the same nominal dimensions as sawn timber, for example 100 x 50 mm, but the surfaces have all been machined to a flat, even width and thickness so that the '100 x 50 mm' timber is actually 91 x 41 mm. The planed sizes of seasoned timber are fairly standard but those of unseasoned timber such as some pines will vary more widely.

Moulded timbers are also ordered by nominal sizes, but check them carefully as once again there will be variations according to the machinery used.

9 Tack the architraves in place with 50 x 2.75 mm lost-head nails through the face of the architrave into the wall and edge of the frame. Do not drive the nails all the way in but leave the heads 5 mm above the surface in case adjustments are needed. This also prevents the hammer marking the surface. Make sure the nails do not protrude through the face of the frame. The nails should be spaced approximately 200–250 mm apart.

10 Place the top architrave upside down on top of the side pieces and mark the required length. Cut the two mitre joints and check the fit. Adjust the architraves as required: if necessary the side pieces may be moved in or out a little to correct the fitting.

11 Apply a little PVA adhesive on the mitre and nail the top architrave to the frame only, not the wall. A nail through the top will help hold the mitre joint tight. Drive in all the nails with a hammer and nail punch, and fill the holes.

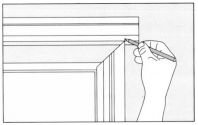

10 Place the top architrave upside down on top of the sides and mark the required length.

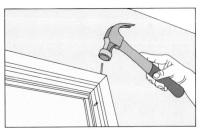

11 Nail the architrave to the frame, not the wall. A nail through the top will help hold the mitre joint tight.

12 When the filler has dried, give it a final sand and apply the required finish to the architraves.

REMOVING SKIRTING

1 Wherever possible start at an external corner or at a join in the skirting. Start with a chisel and lever the board out from the wall. Once it is far enough off the wall, use a crowbar or jemmy behind the skirting to pry it from the wall. Place a block of timber between the crowbar and the wall to prevent damaging the wall. On hollow walls always lever against the wall frame.

2 Repair the wall as necessary by removing any nails and patching the plaster. Sand smooth.

REPLACING SKIRTING

3 Cut the skirting 2 mm over length to allow the joints to push up tight. To cut skirting use a mitre saw or a mitre box and tenon saw.

• To join two lengths of skirting along a wall, use mitred end joints cut at 45 degree angles. Select the skirting piece that will fit behind and cut a mitre on the end to be joined so that the back edge is the longest point of the mitre cut. Tack it in position. Lay the top skirting over the fixed one, with the opposite end already fitted. Mark the long point of the mitre on the face of the top skirting. Cut the mitre and lay the top piece over the first piece, ensuring that the join is tight. Fix it in position (see step 9).

TOOLS AND MATERIALS

• Skirting
• Tape and pencil
• Chisel
• Crowbar or jemmy
• Tenon saw
• Mitre box or mitre saw
• Coping saw or jigsaw
• 50 x 2.5 mm lost-head nails
• Filler

• If an open joint is evident between the skirting and floor, the skirting can be scribed to match the irregularities. Set it in place and run a thin piece of timber along the floor, marking a line the length of the skirting with a sharp pencil. Remove the skirting and plane to the line. Alternatively, fix a small strip of quadrant moulding over the gap.

4 Construct internal corners before external ones. Internal corners usually have one piece of skirting scribed over the other. Take the skirting for one side wall and cut it square to fit tight into the corner of

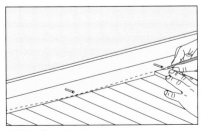

3 To fit skirting over a gap, run a piece of timber and a sharp pencil along the length of the skirting.

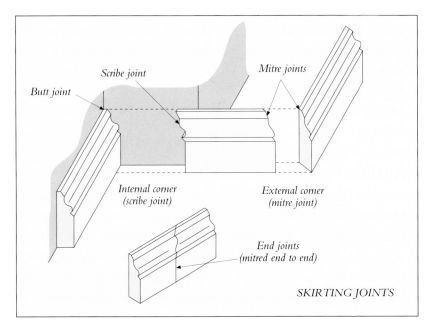

Scribe joint

Mitre joints

Butt joint

Internal corner
(scribe joint)

External corner
(mitre joint)

End joints
(mitred end to end)

SKIRTING JOINTS

the room. Tack it in place with 50 x 2.5 mm lost-head nails. Repeat the process for the skirting on the opposite wall.

5 Take the skirting for the end wall and on the back edge mark off the full length of the wall, ignoring the skirtings that have already been fixed. Cut mitres at these points so that the front is shorter. To complete the joint, use a coping saw or jigsaw to cut along the front edge of the mitre line, square to the face of the skirting. Follow the mitre line as it changes shape across the moulded surface. Check that the joint fits neatly and adjust it as required. Nail the skirtings into position as for architraves (see step 9 on page 20), but using 50 x 2.5 mm nails.

6 For external corners, position the skirting with the internal joint tight and mark the length on the top edge of the skirting at the external corner. This mark represents the internal point of the mitre.

7 Stand the timber on edge in the mitre box or mitre saw. Position the saw blade and check that the angle you are cutting will result in the front face of the skirting being longer than the back. You will need one left-hand and one right-hand 45 degree cut to produce a right-angled external corner.

8 Check the skirtings for fit and adjust them as required. Apply a little PVA adhesive to the mitre joint and secure the skirting (see step 9).

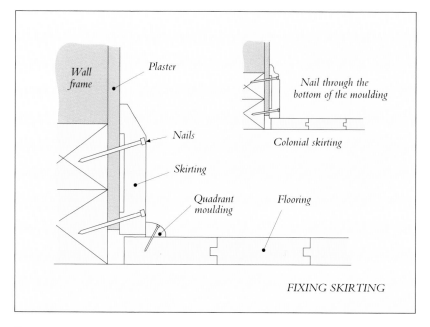

Wall frame

Plaster

Nails

Skirting

Quadrant moulding

Nail through the bottom of the moulding

Colonial skirting

Flooring

FIXING SKIRTING

9 Fix the skirting with 50 x 2.5 mm lost-head nails. You may have to pull the skirting in close, in some areas more than others, thus requiring extra nailing. Leave the heads of the nails above the surface when hammering and finish the job with a nail punch. Drive the nails through the bottom of any moulding where the hole will not be easily seen.

• On hollow walls nail the skirting to the wall frame.

• If fixing to masonry walls, drive the nails through the skirting until they hit the wall. They should be driven hard enough to mark the wall without bending the nails. Remove the skirting. Drill 4 mm holes in the wall with a masonry bit and insert plastic wall plugs. Make sure the plug is flush with the wall before you replace the skirting and fix it into the plastic plugs.

10 Fill the holes and sand smooth. Apply the finish of your choice.

FILLING GAPS

If you do not want to replace your skirting but need to cover a gap between the skirting and the floor, the simplest method is to cover it with a timber strip. Use quadrant moulding and match the timber of the skirting board as closely as possible.

Nail the beading to the floor (*not* the skirting), hammering the nails in at 45 degrees. Mitre the corners so that they sit neatly.

Installing a handrail

Installing or replacing a handrail is not difficult but, if it is to be secure and make a safe stair, it must be done correctly.

COMPONENTS

The handrail itself is supported by newel posts at either end with a balustrade (a series of balusters), which give intermediate support between the posts.

Newel posts (usually at least 90 x 90 mm) are positioned at the top and bottom of each flight. They are fixed to the string (the side support piece of the stairs).

- Usually the posts are centred on the string. If they are installed at the same time as the stairs, a tenon can be cut on the end of the string and a stopped mortise on the bottom of the post so that they lock together. If the post is added after the stair has been installed, a mortise can be cut in the post so it fits over the top of the string (see page 26). In this type of railing the balusters should also be fitted on top of the string.

- A housing can be cut in the post so that it fits beside the string (see page 30). With this type of fixing, the balusters are usually anchored to the outside face of the string. Alternatively, they can be attached to an intermediate rail which runs parallel to the string and the handrail.

Handrails are fixed between the newel posts. They can be fitted to the posts in many ways but the simplest method is with dowel joints.

Balusters are fitted between the handrail and string, not only for support but also for safety. They must not be spaced more than 100 mm apart (when measured horizontally). The balusters can be fixed directly to the string or fitted into a capping moulding that is placed on top of the string.

Turned newel posts and balusters, together with a matching handrail can be purchased in kit form from building suppliers. They come with all the necessary components and fittings ready for installation.

For an elegant result such as this you can purchase turned posts and balusters (and matching handrail) in kit form, but the techniques of installing them are the same as for plain components.

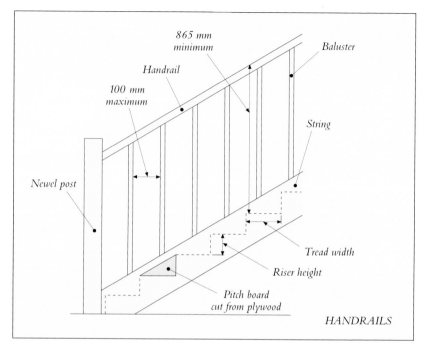

865 mm minimum

Handrail

100 mm maximum

Baluster

String

Newel post

Tread width

Riser height

Pitch board cut from plywood

HANDRAILS

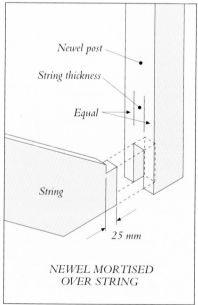

Newel post

String thickness

Equal

String

25 mm

NEWEL MORTISED OVER STRING

NEWEL POST (FIXED OVER STRING)

1 Begin with the bottom post. Measure 25 mm in from the end of the string along the bottom and draw a vertical line up the outside of the string. Square the line across the edge and back down the inside face of the string.

2 Place a square on the end of the string and square a line back from the corner to the vertical line. Use a tenon saw to cut the small triangular section off the corner.

3 Set out a 25 mm deep mortise in the centre of the post to receive the end of the string. Make it as wide as

the string thickness. Use a marking gauge to scribe the set-out lines parallel to the edge. Lay the post on a solid flat surface and then chisel out the mortise.

4 Fit the post over the string. Drill two 4 mm screw holes through the post 12 mm from the edge. Then counterbore the holes so the screw heads will finish below the surface. Use a spirit level to check that the post is vertical, and secure it with 65 mm x 8 gauge countersunk screws. Cut timber plugs to fill the holes and sand smooth.

5 Take the top post and set out a mortise to fit over the string. Cut the bottom of the post so it sits flat on the floor. Ensure the top is the same height above the string as the top of the bottom post.

6 Fix the top post with screws through the side into the string in the same manner as the bottom post. In addition, fix a screw through the floor from underneath or skew it through the back and plug it with

timber. Alternatively, a dowel drilled into the floor and the bottom of the post will provide good strength.

FIXING THE HANDRAIL

7 Set out the height of the handrail on the post at 865 mm minimum above the front edge of the tread. Square a line across the face of the post above the string. This is the top of the handrail.

8 Use a sliding bevel or pitch board (see diagram opposite) to set out the angles and cut the handrail to fit between the newel posts on top of the string (see diagram on page 28).

9 At each end of the handrail, set out the positions for two dowels, 50 mm long and 10 mm in diameter, 13 mm in from the narrowest part of the rail.

10 Place a 10 mm dowelling bit in an electric drill and carefully bore 25 mm deep holes square to the cut.

11 Place a dowel centre in each hole and centre the handrail against the posts, under the squared line. Have a

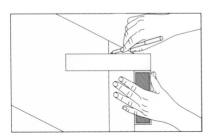

2 Place a square on the end of the string and square a line back from the corner to the plumb line.

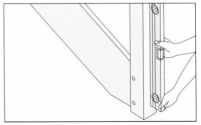

4 Fit the post over the string, check that it is vertical, and secure it with 65 mm x 8 gauge countersunk screws.

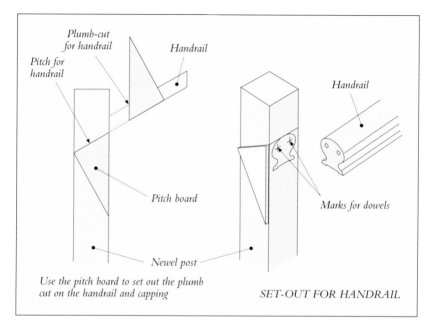

Plumb-cut for handrail

Pitch for handrail

Handrail

Pitch board

Marks for dowels

Newel post

Handrail

Use the pitch board to set out the plumb cut on the handrail and capping

SET-OUT FOR HANDRAIL

second person hold the other end up at the correct height while you align the handrail. Press the joint together to mark the centres on the posts. Remove the handrail and dowel centres. Bore the corresponding holes in the posts 28 mm deep.

12 Place a little PVA adhesive into the dowel holes and on the end of

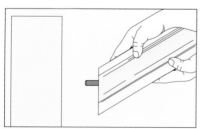

12 Place the handrail in position between the posts, bringing the bottom joint together first.

the handrail. Insert the dowels into the handrail. Place it in position between the posts, bringing the bottom joint together first. Lower the other end of the handrail and push down, spreading the top post a little to spring the rail into position.

13 Remove any excess adhesive with a damp rag. If required, add a screw underneath the handrail into the joint on the bottom post. Although it is difficult to add one to the top joint without it being seen, extra strength can be added by screwing through the back of the post. Alternatively, you can try nailing through the top or side of the handrail into the post. Punch the nails in and fill over them or use a timber plug to camouflage the hole.

STAIR MAINTENANCE

Stairs generally don't require maintenance unless they've been damaged but some timber may shrink or wear slightly, especially the treads, causing the stair to squeak as it is used.

1 Identify the tread that is squeaking by moving along the

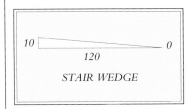

10   0
120
STAIR WEDGE

stair slowly and rocking back and forth a little at each tread.

2 From underneath, tighten the screws and repunch any nails.

3 Use a hammer to drive in the wedges that hold the treads and rises in the housings. Replace any split, broken or missing wedges. Wedges are cut at a pitch of 1:12 and should support the whole tread. Clean out the housing with a chisel. Apply a little PVA adhesive to the wedge and drive it in until it is firm.

FIXING THE BALUSTERS

14 Trim each end of the capping moulding to match the top of the string. Fix it in place by nailing through the groove into the top of the string.

15 Calculate the number of balusters required and their spacing by taking the horizontal measurement between the posts and subtracting the maximum allowed spacing. Then divide this by the same spacing plus the width of one baluster (usually 40 mm). For example:
Horizontal measurement (2072 mm) minus maximum spacing (100 mm) = 1972 mm
Maximum spacing (100 mm) plus width of one baluster (40 mm) = 140 mm

Number of balusters = 1972 divided by 140 = 14
The spacing between balusters = horizontal measurement minus the width of 14 balusters, divided by 15 (one more than the number of balusters).
2072 mm − 560 = 1492 divided by 15 spacings = 99.4 mm (rounded up to 100 mm)

16 Take a small scrap piece of timber and make a spacer to match the spacing.

17 Use the pitch template to mark the bevel on the bottom and top of each baluster. Cut them to length, taking care that the bevel is cut the correct way around so that they fit neatly under the rail.

29

NEWEL POST FIXED BESIDE THE STRING

An alternative method of erecting the post is to fix it beside the string. This method is suitable when you are adding a post to an existing string.

1 Cut the posts to the required height. Hold the post vertical and use a spirit level against the side of the post. Mark the pitch (angle) of the top of the string on the side of the post. This will represent the top shoulder of the housing.

2 Cramp the post to a pair of trestles and mark a cross where the joint will be cut. Square the shoulder lines across each side. Set a marking gauge to 25 mm and mark a line from the square lines down the post. Continue the lines across the bottom.

3 Use a saw to cut straight across the housing several times, in order to break the grain. Carefully chisel out the housing.

4 Cramp the post in position and check that it is vertical both ways. Adjust the housing as required. Secure the post with two 12 mm diameter roundhead bolts. You may counterbore the bolt heads and fill the holes with timber plugs. If there is no access under the stairs use coach screws. Repeat for all posts, ensuring all the posts finish the same height above the string.

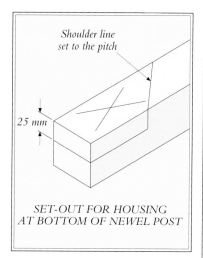

Shoulder line set to the pitch

25 mm

SET-OUT FOR HOUSING
AT BOTTOM OF NEWEL POST

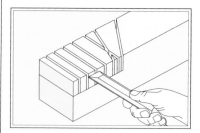

3 Use a saw to cut across the housing several times to break the grain. Chisel out the housing.

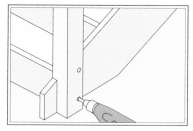

4 If desired, counterbore the heads of the bolts and fill the holes with matching timber plugs.

18 While fitting each baluster, use the spacer to support the timber as you nail through the baluster into the capping moulding and handrail in turn. Fix about half the balusters and then check that they are vertical and parallel. Adjust them as necessary and continue checking as you complete the balustrade.

19 On the landing balustrades are fixed into the handrail by skew nailing into the groove underneath. On the floor, either fix them into a capping piece nailed to the floor or dowel the ends of the balusters into the floor.

20 If desired, bevel cut the ends of a small moulding to fit into the groove in the capping moulding between each baluster. Fix it with 18 mm panel pins into the groove.

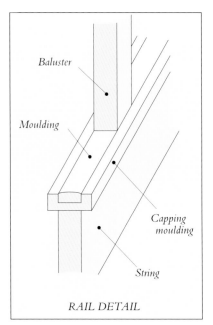

Baluster

Moulding

Capping moulding

String

RAIL DETAIL

21 Fill any nail holes and sand them smooth. Apply the finish of your choice according to the instructions.

CUTTING TIMBER TO LENGTH

In carpentry projects you often need to cut timber precisely so the item is symmetrical and square.

1 Use a try square to square a line across the timber close to the end, ensuring that any splits or chips will be removed.

2 Using a bench hook to hold the timber steady, cut on the waste side of the line. (The bench hook has a batten that hooks onto the front of the workbench and another to hold the timber steady.)

3 Using a tape and pencil, measure off the required length from this squared end. Cut on the waste side of the line.

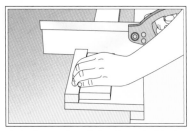

2 Using a bench hook to hold the timber steady, cut on the waste side of the line.

Plumbing or other pipes running down a wall (inset) can present an unsightly appearance, but a box frame can be built around them to camouflage them.

Concealing a pipe

It is not difficult to hide an exposed pipe with a neat pilaster. Simply fix battens to the wall and attach panels to them.

FIXING THE BATTENS

1 The pilaster should be kept clear of the pipe as the pipe may shift over time or vibrate in the case of a water pipe. Place a square on the floor and slide it along the wall until the blade touches the pipe. At the end of the blade mark a line on the wall with a pencil. Repeat on the other side and measure 20 mm out from these marks. Check along the pipe for any joints or other pipes that connect into the main line. These may influence where the panelling is fixed. If they extend out more than 20 mm (the clearance allowed), move the starting mark out to suit. You can cut the panels to fit around any intersecting pipes.

2 Use a spirit level and pencil to make a vertical line the full height of the wall.

3 Cut two 50 x 25 mm timber battens to fit the full height of the wall. You may need to cut them short to clear the cornice or skirting.

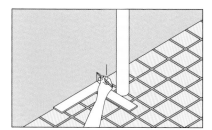

1 Place a square on the floor and slide it along the wall until the blade touches the pipe. Mark the wall.

2 Allowing 20 mm clearance, use a spirit level and pencil to draw a vertical line the height of the wall.

4 Fix the battens to the wall.

• If the wall is timber framed, fix the battens firmly to the studs or noggings within the wall. Locate these with a stud finder or by tapping the wall lightly with your hand or hammer and listening for the solid sound. Mark where you think the studs are with a pencil. Lightly tap a fine-gauge nail into the spot to confirm. Transfer these marks to the batten. Lay the batten down on a trestle and at each mark drill a 5 mm hole through the timber. Reposition the batten against the wall on the vertical line. Use a 3.5 mm bit and drill through the holes in the batten and 25 mm into the wall.

• Fix battens to masonry walls by using a nylon drive-pin plug, either round-head or countersunk. Position the batten on the trestles as before

and drill 6.5 mm holes through the timber, approximately 300–450 mm apart. Reposition the batten on the wall against the vertical line. Then, using a 6.5 mm tungsten-tipped masonry bit, drill 30mm into the wall through these holes. Once you have marked the wall with the drill bit, remove the batten to make the job easier. Check the holes for depth. If they are correct, position the batten and insert the drive pins. Check that the batten is vertical and drive the pins in with a hammer.

ADDING THE PANELLING

5 Make the side panels wide enough to allow 20 mm clearance round the pipe (see the diagram below). The front panel width is the overall spacing of the battens plus 32 mm (the thickness of the side panels). Set

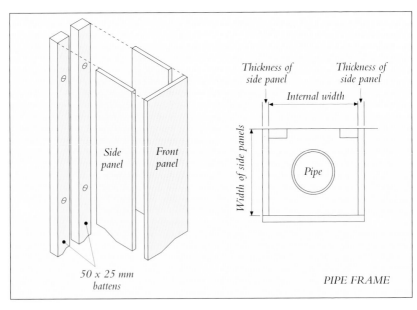

Side panel

Front panel

50 x 25 mm battens

Thickness of side panel

Thickness of side panel

Internal width

Width of side panels

Pipe

PIPE FRAME

the circular saw guide to cut slightly over the finished width of the side and front panels. Lay the MDF on a pair of trestles and rip the board, taking care to cut straight. When cutting MDF, be sure to wear a dust mask and safety glasses as well as hearing protection. Clean up the edge with a hand plane.

6 Cut the panels to fit between the floor and ceiling. The side panels may need to be shaped to fit over the skirting and cornice. If so, cut a thin piece of cardboard to match the profile of the cornice or skirting. Place this template against the cornice and check for fit. Adjust as required. Position the template on the side panel and trace around it with a sharp pencil. Cut the shape with a jigsaw. Test the fit by positioning each side in place. If preferred, the skirting can be cut away to allow the panel to fit flush against the wall.

7 Lay the side panels flat on trestles and drill a 5 mm hole through each panel 10 mm in from the wall edge and at approximately 300 mm intervals. Countersink each hole to receive the screws. Position the panel against the batten and drill through each hole with a 3 mm bit into the batten, ensuring the panel is hard against the wall. Secure with 30 mm x 8 gauge screws.

8 Fix the front panel to the edges of the side panels in the same manner.

Drill the clearance holes 8 mm in from the edges and countersink each as before. Keep the edge of the front panel in line with the face of the side panels. Drill the pilot holes and fasten with the screws.

TO FINISH
9 Give the pilaster a light sand and paint it to match the walls.

HINT

If you may require access to the pipe, you can cut a removable section in one panel. This will be easier than having to remove the whole panel. Make two square cuts across the panel to make an access hole, then replace the section and fix it through the face with screws.

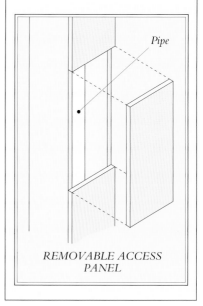

Pipe

REMOVABLE ACCESS
PANEL

Old insect damage is visible in patches on these otherwise attractive floorboards. Using the method given in this project, the affected parts can be replaced without re-laying the whole floor.

Repairing timber floors

Timber floors are beautiful to look at, easy to clean and cheap to maintain. Damaged boards can easily be replaced without re-laying the whole floor.

MATERIALS AND TOOLS

- Floorboards to match existing ones
- 50 x 2.5 mm lost-head or twisted-shank nails
- 50 x 50 mm batten, 75 x 2.75 mm lost-head nails (optional)
- Abrasive paper
- Pencil
- Claw hammer
- Tenon or circular saw
- Drill and keyhole saw or jigsaw (optional)
- Firmer chisel
- Chisel: 6 mm bevel-edge
- Nail punch
- Cork block or electric sander

DAMAGED FLOORS

Timber floors can be damaged in a number of ways and they may then be quite dangerous. In addition, split or broken boards can creak very annoyingly every time somebody walks over them.

When floors are damaged by rot or decay, usually caused by damp, the underlying problem must be remedied before the floor is repaired (see the box on page 39). Beetle or other insect damage should be treated by a licensed pest controller.

Many floors can be made sound and attractive again simply by replacing one or two boards and repunching the nails. If the repair is on the edge of the floor, near the wall, the skirting will normally have to be taken up and replaced when the flooring has been relaid. It is sometimes easier to replace a whole board than part of one.

REMOVING DAMAGED FLOORING

1 Locate the floor joist closest to the damage and mark its width and direction on the floor with a pencil. To find the joist, look for existing nail holes (usually near the centre of the joist) or climb under the floor and measure off from a wall (allow

---

SQUEAKY BOARDS

If you have a problem with a squeaking floorboard that is otherwise quite sound, it can be fixed by screwing a batten under it. Working from underneath the floor, use synthetic resin adhesive and 30 mm screws to fix a 50 x 25 mm batten across the width of the offending board.

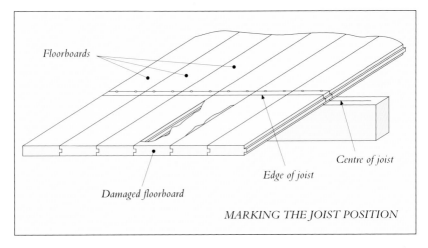

Floorboards

Centre of joist

Edge of joist

Damaged floorboard

MARKING THE JOIST POSITION

for any wall linings). Alternatively, from below the floor, drill a hole through the damaged floorboard and measure back to the joist from this hole. Transfer this measurement to the top of the floor. If you can't get under the floor, you can gain an idea of where the joists are by gently tapping the floor with a hammer and listening for the change in sound. A definite solid sound can be detected whenever you hit a joist.

2 Cut the damaged floorboards across either directly beside the

vertical edge of the joist or on the centre of the joist. It may be easier to remove two or three boards rather than just one. Cut both ends of the boards to be removed.

• To cut the boards in the centre of the joist, use a tenon saw and cut on the waste side of the centre line. If you are removing several boards, use a circular saw. You can also use a firmer chisel driven with a sharp blow from a mallet to cut through the board 5 mm on the waste side of the line. Once the board is removed, use the chisel to cut back to the line.

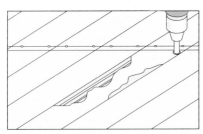

2 To cut beside the joint, drill a 10 mm hole through the damaged board to clear the edge of the joist.

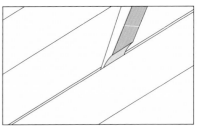

4 Lever out the damaged board with a firmer chisel. Take care not to break the tongue that is to remain.

HINT

Where possible, take a sample of your flooring to your supplier to match the existing boards. If your local supplier can't match them, try a timber recycler or buy planed timber and re-run the tongue and groove yourself.

You can also remove boards from a less conspicuous part of the room or another room.

• To cut beside the joist, drill a 10 mm hole through the damaged floorboard beside the set-out line so that it clears the edge of the joist. Place the blade of a keyhole saw or jigsaw through the hole and cut along the edge of the joist.

3 Use the tenon saw or jigsaw to cut along the damaged board to split off the tongue. Make sure you cut the tongue on the damaged board only, not the boards that are to remain.

4 Punch any nails through and lever out the damaged board with a firmer chisel. Be careful not to break the tongue on the floorboard that is to remain in place.

5 To remove the split tongue from the groove of the other remaining floorboard, drive a 6 mm chisel horizontally into the groove at each end of the hole. This should cut the tongue. Then lever out the waste. Check that the groove is now completely clear.

CAUSES OF DAMP

• The main cause of damp is poor ventilation, especially common in older houses. It can be improved by clearing existing vents of dirt or vegetation to allow free flow of air. In some cases, additional or larger vents may have to be cut through the outside wall.
• Leaking taps or pipes, blocked or broken waste or overflow pipes, or even poorly installed appliances such as washing machines or dishwashers can create a damp problem. Check all pipes under the floor or close by for leaks. Have any repairs required carried out.
• Faulty flashings or damp-proof courses can allow water to filter into adjacent floors.
• You may need to install agricultural drains in gardens directly against the house so that any excess water is directed away from the house.

6 Cut a 50 x 50 mm batten to fit beside the joist to support the new floor (see the diagram on page 40). Secure it with 75 x 2.75 mm lost-head nails every 150 mm.

REPLACING FLOORBOARDS
7 Measure and cut the new boards. Slightly undercut the ends so that you will be able to wedge them in tightly. Remove the bottom edge of the groove with a chisel or saw to produce a rebate.

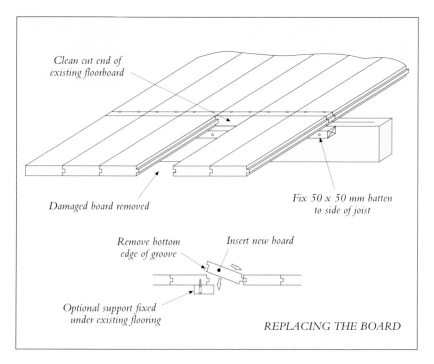

Clean cut end of existing floorboard

Damaged board removed

Fix 50 x 50 mm batten to side of joist

Remove bottom edge of groove

Insert new board

Optional support fixed under existing flooring

REPLACING THE BOARD

8 If you think it is necessary, fix a support under the tongue side of the existing flooring to help prevent the joint creaking.

9 Fit the new floorboard into the gap. Tap it down firmly and check that it fits neatly. If necessary, remove it and adjust the fit.

10 Drill two 2 mm pilot holes through the boards at each joist and/or batten to receive the 50 x 2.5 mm lost-head nails. These holes should be angled slightly to increase the holding power of the nails, or use twisted-shank nails. Hammer in the nails and then centre-punch them below the surface.

11 Sand the face down to finish flush with the original floor. Fill the nail holes with filler that matches the timber and apply the finish of your choice. Replace any skirting or architraves that were removed.

REPLACING DECKING

To remove a rotten decking board cut the ends over joists and lever up the board with a crowbar. Be careful to pull out all the nails. Measure the section to be replaced and cut a new board to span at least three joists. Fit it in place and fix with two 50 mm twist-shanked nails into the joists at each end. Punch in the nails.

MAKING A PET DOOR

Pet doors need to swing both in and out. The door should be big enough to be comfortable for your pet but not big enough to allow inclement weather or unwanted intruders to enter your home.

For the pet door frame you will need 50 x 25 mm PAR timber and for the architrave 50 x 19 mm PAR. The flap can be 6 mm waterproof plywood or clear plastic.

1 Work out the size of the opening your pet will need and add 18 mm on all sides for the frame lining. Use a square and pencil to mark the opening on the door, making sure it is above the bottom frame.

2 Drill a 10 mm hole through the door in each corner of the set-out. Cut along the line with a jigsaw. In a hollow door, fix battens between the panels.

3 Measure the thickness of the door and use a marking gauge to draw a matching line on the pet door frame. Plane back to the gauge line.

4 Cut the two vertical pieces to fit. Sand them to remove sharp corners. Apply primer to the back face and fix them in place with 40 x 2.5 mm galvanised lost-head nails, ensuring both edges are flush with the face of the door.

5 Cut the two horizontal pieces. On the bottom one plane a slight bevel halfway across the top face so that any water will drain outwards. On the top one cut a 6 x 4 mm drip groove 5 mm in from the front edge. Fix these pieces in place as for the vertical pieces.

6 Mitre architrave around the opening on the inside and outside, leaving 4 mm of the frame exposed. Coat the edges of the frame and back of the architrave with primer, and then nail the architrave in place.

7 Cut a door flap, making it 10 mm smaller all round than the opening. Plane a slight bevel on the top edge to prevent it catching as it swings. Then, sand and apply a coat of primer.

8 Screw two 100 mm T-hinges on the top piece, 25 mm in from each side. Position the flap in the centre of the opening with the bevel at the top, and mark the hinge positions on it. Remove the door and drill holes using a 5 mm twist bit. Fix the flap in place with nuts and machine screws.

9 Apply the finish of your choice and, if desired, add a self-adhesive weather seal around the opening and a magnetic catch.

Timber insect screen

Although they are most common in warmer countries, insect meshes are becoming increasingly popular in Western Europe, and are ideal for protecting the home from unwanted intruders!

MATERIALS★			
PART	MATERIAL	FINISHED LENGTH	No.
Stile	50 x 25 mm timber PAR	1424 mm	2
Top/bottom rail	50 x 25 mm timber PAR	874 mm	2
Intermediate rail	38 x 25 mm timber PAR	864 mm	1

OTHER: Epoxy adhesive; ten 8 mm diameter 50 mm long dowels; abrasive paper: 120 grit; 1 x 1.5 m black nylon insect mesh; 5 m plastic spline; finish of choice

★ Makes one screen 1424 x 954 mm to fit an opening 1430 x 960 mm. Timber sizes given are nominal. For timber types, see the box on page 20.

INSECT SCREENS

Traditional insect screens are made from timber with screen mesh stretched across the face. There are two main methods of holding the mesh in place.

• The mesh is stapled to the frame and a decorative beading is fixed over the top to prevent the edge fraying. Follow steps 1–11 and then staple mesh to the frame and fix beading over the edge.

• A groove is run in the face of the frame, the mesh is pushed into the groove and a spline (plastic tubing) is pushed in as a wedge.

The screen may be held in place with barrel bolts, turn buckles or similar means, or it may be screwed to the window frame itself. Whatever method you choose, the screen should be held firmly enough not to rattle in the wind. You should be able to remove the screen from the window easily for regular cleaning and maintenance.

The screen can be fitted over the face of a window or sit within its frame. However, make sure that this does not impede the operation of the window itself.

MEASURING UP

1 You can work out which materials will be needed by measuring the size of the window opening between the lining. A clearance of 3 mm on all sides is required, slightly bigger if the screen will be painted. For example, if the opening measures 1430 x 960 mm, the frame size should be 1424 x 954 mm.

This timber insect screen is constructed from western red cedar for its light weight and high durability. The mesh is inserted into a groove cut around the face of the frame.

TOOLS

- Tape measure and pencil
- Tenon saw
- Mitre box or mitre saw (optional)
- Marking gauge
- Try square
- Combination square
- Dowel jig (optional)
- Electric drill
- Drill bits: 8 mm, dowelling, countersink
- Hammer
- G-cramps and sash cramps
- Electric router (6 mm straight bit)
- Chisel
- Hand plane
- Craft knife
- Spline roller

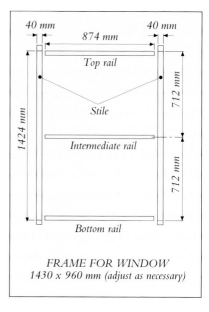

FRAME FOR WINDOW
1430 x 960 mm (adjust as necessary)

set-out lines. Using a mitre box or mitre saw will ensure an accurate cut.

2 Measure the rails (horizontal pieces) to the finished length, that is, the overall width of the frame less the width of the stiles (954 − 80 = 874 mm) and square a pencil line around all sides. Cut them to length using a tenon saw, ensuring you cut square and on the waste side of the

JOINT CONSTRUCTION

3 The rails are fixed to the stiles with timber dowels. There are two dowels in each joint in the top and bottom rails and one in each intermediate rail joint. On the ends of the top and bottom rails mark the centre lines for the two dowels, 9.5 mm in from

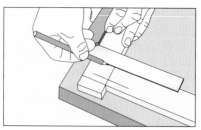

4 Lay the pieces face up and, using a try square, transfer the centre lines from the rails to the stiles.

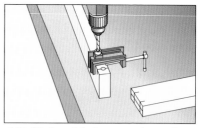

5 Drill dowel holes at each mark on both rails and stiles, using a metal dowelling jig if you have one.

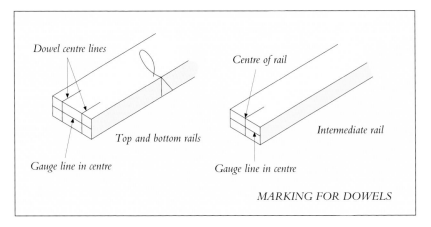

Dowel centre lines

Centre of rail

Top and bottom rails

Intermediate rail

Gauge line in centre

Gauge line in centre

MARKING FOR DOWELS

each edge. Continue the lines up and onto the faces of the rails. Using the marking gauge, draw a line across the middle to form two intersecting marks. Then use the marking gauge on the intermediate rail to draw a line across the ends. Measure the width of the intermediate rail and mark the centre. Square this line across the ends and the faces.

4 Mark the required length on the stiles (vertical pieces) and square a line around the timber at each point. Lay each stile and rail face up on a flat surface in their correct positions. Using a try square, transfer the centre lines from the rails onto the stiles. Number and mark each joint in turn. The intermediate rail should be in the centre of the stiles.

5 Drill dowel holes 8 mm in diameter and 28 mm deep (half the length of the dowel plus a little clearance) at each mark on both rails and stiles.

6 Countersink the top of each hole to remove any fibres. To test for accuracy, assemble the frame before gluing. Check that it is square and the correct size.

7 Place adhesive in the dowel holes and on the surface of the joint. Insert the dowels into the rails and tap them home with a hammer (protect the timber with a scrap block). Fix the rails to one stile. Add on the other stile. Wipe off excess adhesive.

8 Place the frame in the sash cramps. You will need to use three cramps –

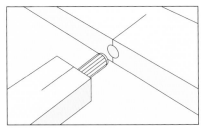

*7 **Apply adhesive in the holes, insert the dowels into the rails and fit them to one stile.***

one for each rail. Apply an even pressure to close up the joints. The cramps should be placed square and parallel to the work. They must also be positioned so that they are in line with each rail.

9 Check the rails are parallel. Although you will be able to make slight adjustments, remember that very little movement can be obtained with this type of joint. Measure the diagonals. If they are the same, then the job is square. If not, a sharp tap on the end of the stile may move it enough. If necessary, adjust the cramps to bring it into square.

10 Check across the top for flatness. Then, tap any joints that are not flat with a hammer (use a block of timber to protect the joint). If the joint does not flatten, you may need to ease the cramp off a little, or cramp a piece of timber across it. Sight across the rails and adjust the frame as required to remove any twist before it dries. Again, remove any excess adhesive before finally leaving the job to dry.

11 Trim the stiles to length and plane or sand the face of the joints flush. Check the fit of the frame and plane it lightly if necessary. Some windows have a splay on the sill. If yours does, match it on the bottom of the frame.

FITTING THE SCREEN
12 The screen is held in place by a plastic spline (wedge) inserted into a groove in the face of the frame. Use a combination square as a pencil gauge to mark a line for the edge of the groove 26 mm in from the outside edge all round the face side (see the diagram opposite). Place a 6 mm straight bit into a router to cut a groove 6 mm deep. Set the fence on the router to cut the groove.

13 Using G-cramps, hold the frame down while you rout the groove. At the right-hand end of one side, hold the router with the fence against the outside edge of the frame. Turn it on and lower it into the face. Run the groove along the frame, stopping at the pencil gauge lines. Repeat this on all four sides of the frame, taking care

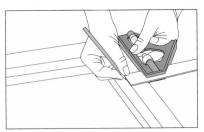

12 Use a combination square to mark a line all round the face side to represent the edge of the groove.

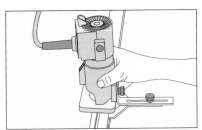

13 Hold the router with the fence against the outside edge of the frame and run the groove along the frame.

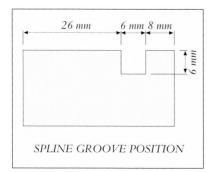

26 mm   6 mm 8 mm

6 mm

SPLINE GROOVE POSITION

not to run past the lines. Clean out the groove with a chisel.

14 Sand the frame and remove any sharp edges with 120 grit abrasive paper. Apply paint to match the window, or you can use paint in a contrasting colour.

15 Lay the frame flat on a table with the grooved face up. Roll the screen over the face of the frame as close as you can to square so that it covers the whole frame. Starting at one corner, push the plastic spline into the groove using the spline roller. This will wedge the screen into the groove. Take care to keep the screen even to avoid wrinkles or creases

developing. If it does wrinkle, pull the spline up and start again. Work around all sides of the frame, pulling the screen as you go to keep the tension even.

16 Cut the spline to length when near the end and complete the job. Trim off all excess screen by cutting on the outside edge of the groove with a craft knife.

17 To hold the screen in place, screw a U-section of aluminium under the top lining of the window. The top of the screen is then slipped up inside it. The bottom section of the screen can be held firmly with two barrel bolts, installed either on the outside or the inside, where they are less obvious.

HINT

PVA adhesive is adequate for an insect screen, provided the finished job is painted. For a better job, use a water-resistant adhesive such as epoxy resin.

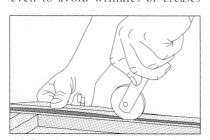

15 Starting at one corner, push the plastic spline into the groove using the spline roller.

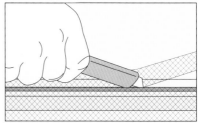

16 Trim off all excess screen by cutting on the outside edge of the groove with a craft knife.

Basic shelf

This simple shelf has been made from medium-density fibreboard (MDF), with the shelf itself of one thickness and the brackets made from two thicknesses of board glued together.

MATERIALS*				
PART	MATERIAL	FINISHED LENGTH	WIDTH	NO.
Bracket	16 mm MDF	150 mm	200 mm	2
Shelf	16 mm MDF	750 mm	150 mm	1

OTHER: PVA adhesive; abrasive paper: one sheet of 120 grit; four 25 mm long 8 mm diameter dowels and dowel centres; four 65 mm x 8 gauge countersunk chipboard screws; finish of choice

* Finished size: 150 mm wide and 750 mm long.

A SIMPLE SHELF

MDF makes a shelf suitable for most situations. To create a more solid shelf, glue together two thicknesses of board. Solid timber could be substituted, if preferred, or metal brackets could be used.

The length of the shelf can be adjusted as necessary but there should be an overhang of 50–75 mm at each end. If the shelf is over 1 m long, place another bracket in the centre.

CAUTION

Medium-density fibreboard contains chemicals that can cause skin problems in some people. Always work out of the sun, wear gloves and protect your nose, mouth and lungs from the dust.

Several shelves can be fixed one above the other.

MAKING THE BRACKETS

1 Using a square, tape and pencil, mark out two 200 x 150 mm pieces of MDF. Cut them with a panel saw.

2 Apply PVA adhesive evenly over the face of one piece. Lay the other on the adhesive and rub it around to spread the adhesive and remove air. Suction will hold the pieces together. Check the joint and if there are gaps squeeze the joint up with G-cramps. Keep the edges in alignment while the adhesive dries. Wipe off excess adhesive with a damp rag.

3 Hold the double piece upright in a vice and plane one edge straight and square. Use a square to mark off a

The length of this neat little shelf can be adjusted to suit, with extra brackets added as necessary. It will find many uses in the home.

squared corner at one end of this edge and plane it back to the line. Mark the squared corner with a cross. Turn the piece around and repeat the process to produce another squared corner diagonally opposite the first.

4 Measure 145 mm along each edge from the squared corners and square a line on the face. Use a combination

4 Use a combination square and pencil to mark lines parallel to the measured off edges and 30 mm in.

TOOLS

- Combination square
- Tape and pencil
- Panel saw
- Spreader
- G-cramps
- Vice
- Hand plane
- 150 mm diameter plate and smaller tin or cup
- Jigsaw
- Half-round second cut file
- Electric drill
- Drill bits: 3 mm, 8 mm, 8 mm twist bit, countersink
- Spirit level
- Screwdriver

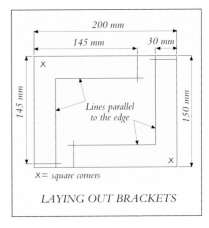

LAYING OUT BRACKETS

square and pencil to mark lines parallel to the measured off edges and 30 mm in (see the diagram above).

5 Position a 150 mm diameter plate in the corner of the 'L' shape and trace around it with a pencil.

6 Select a smaller round object, position it on the 145 mm mark and

the end of the concave curve. Trace around it for the end curves. Ensure that the curves flow smoothly.

7 Cut along the waste side of the line with a jigsaw. Clean up with a half-round second cut file and abrasive paper. The edge can be shaped with a router or abrasive paper. Repeat steps 1–7 for the second bracket (more if required).

ASSEMBLING THE SHELF

8 Cut out the shelf. If desired, mark and cut a curve on the two front ends to match the brackets.

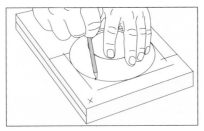

5 To produce the curved shape for the bracket, position a plate in the corner of the 'L' shape and trace around it.

6 Trace around a smaller round object to produce the convex curve on the end of the bracket.

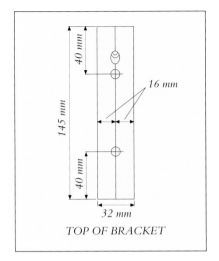

40 mm

145 mm

40 mm

16 mm

32 mm

TOP OF BRACKET

9 Decide how you will fix the shelf to the wall (see the diagrams on pages 52 and 53). If you have a timber frame wall, fix the brackets directly to the studs (450 or 600 mm apart).

10 On top of each bracket, measure in from each end 40 mm; square a line across. For the dowel centres, set a marking gauge to 16 mm and mark a line along the centre.

11 Drill an 8 mm hole 20 mm deep at each location. Place masking tape

around the drill bit to indicate the depth required.

12 Lay the shelf face down on a flat surface and measure in an even amount from each end for the overhang. Square a line across for the outside face of each bracket.

13 Place a dowel centre in each hole on the brackets. Place the brackets on the squared lines on the shelf with the back edges flush. Push down firmly to mark the dowel positions.

14 Drill the holes 8 mm deep, taking care not to drill right through the shelf. Use masking tape as before to indicate the depth on the drill bit.

FIXING TO THE WALL
15 About 30 mm up from the bottom of the bracket, drill a 4.5 mm hole through the bracket at 90 degrees to the back. Drill another hole at 45 degrees through the top to come out through the back.

16 Mark the positions of the top of the brackets on the wall, using a

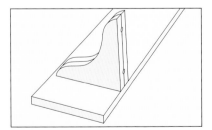

13 Place the bracket on the shelf with the back edges flush and push it down firmly to mark the dowel positions.

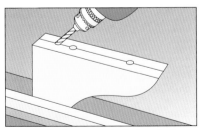

15 Drill the second fixing hole at 45 degrees through the top to come out through the back.

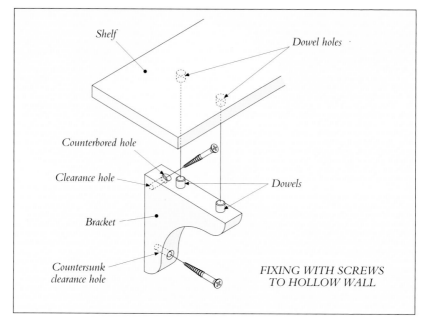

Shelf

Dowel holes

Counterbored hole

Clearance hole

Dowels

Bracket

Countersunk
clearance hole

*FIXING WITH SCREWS
TO HOLLOW WALL*

spirit level to ensure they are level. Measure up and mark the thickness of the shelf and the overhangs at each end. From these two points mark a vertical line down the wall for the outside edge of each bracket.

17 Hold the bracket on the wall, insert a 65 mm screw through each hole and tap with a hammer. The

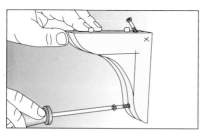

18 Countersink or counterbore the screw holes. Position each bracket and fix it with the screws.

point of the screw will mark the wall. Remove the bracket and drill a 3 mm hole at these marks (the top hole is angled). For a masonry wall use a 6.5 mm tungsten-tipped drill bit and plastic wall plug.

18 On the brackets countersink the bottom hole to take the screw head and counterbore the top hole with an 8 mm twist bit so the screw head will finish below the surface. Position each bracket and fix with the screws.

TO FINISH
19 Lay the shelf on the brackets and locate it on the dowels. Add a little adhesive to the holes if required.

20 Apply a coat of primer/sealer and two coats of paint of your choice.

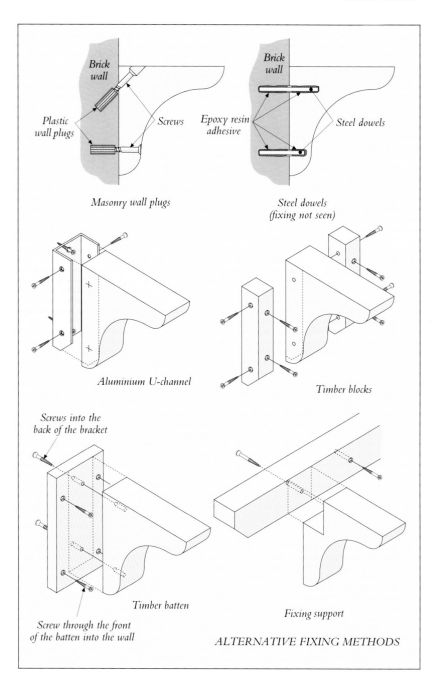

Brick
wall

Plastic
wall plugs

Screws

Masonry wall plugs

Brick
wall

Epoxy resin
adhesive

Steel dowels

Steel dowels
(fixing not seen)

Aluminium U-channel

Timber blocks

Screws into the
back of the bracket

Timber batten

Screw through the front
of the batten into the wall

Fixing support

ALTERNATIVE FIXING METHODS

A built-in cupboard can provide much-needed storage space by fitting neatly across a room or into an alcove. Sliding doors across the front from floor to ceiling and wall to wall ensure a neat and stylish look.

Built-in cupboard

This built-in cupboard with sliding doors is designed to incorporate several different types of storage. The configuration can be altered to suit your particular needs.

	MATERIALS★			
PART	MATERIAL	FINISHED LENGTH	WIDTH	NO.
Divider	16 mm white melamine	1800 mm	450 mm	4
Shelf	16 mm white melamine	387 mm	450 mm	10
Long shelf	16 mm white melamine	790 mm	450 mm	1
Top shelf	16 mm white melamine	2386 mm	450 mm	1
Side piece	16 mm white melamine	300 mm	450 mm	2
Bench	16 mm chipboard	790 mm	450 mm	1
Reinforcement	16 mm chipboard	790 mm	50 mm	1
Bench support	25 x 25 mm timber PAR	450 mm		2
Reveal head	125 x 25 mm timber PAR	2386 mm		1
Side reveal	125 x 25 mm timber PAR	2400 mm		2
Middle rail	100 x 38 mm timber PAR	2400 mm		1
Bulkhead	90 x 35 mm pine	2400 mm		2
Bulkhead stud	90 x 35 mm pine	130 mm		5
Int. architrave	75 x 25 mm timber PAR	2400 mm		3
Ext. architrave	75 x 25 mm architrave	2400 mm		3
Pelmet	75 x 25 mm timber PAR	2400 mm		1

OTHER: Eight 25 mm dowels and dowel centres; 50 mm x 8 gauge countersunk chipboard screws; 25 mm x 8 gauge countersunk chipboard screws; 25 x 2 mm nails; 75 x 3.5 mm lost-head nails; 65 x 2.75 mm lost-head nails; PVA adhesive; contact adhesive; abrasive paper: 120 grit; 900 x 600 mm plastic laminate; plasterboard; cornice; four 1800 x 600 mm doors; four 18 mm thick 600 x 450 mm doors; two 2400 mm sliding door track kits; panel pins

★Finished size: This cupboard (without top storage) was 1816 mm high, 2386 mm long and 450 mm deep. Adjust the size to fit your room; for use as a wardrobe make it 600 mm deep. Timber sizes given are nominal (see page 20).

TOOLS

- Tape and pencil
- Builders square
- Circular saw with fine teeth
- Panel saw
- Tenon saw
- Mitre saw
- Electric drill
- Drill bits: 4.5 mm, 5 mm, 8 mm dowelling
- Dowelling jig
- G-cramps
- Spirit level
- Hand plane
- Hammer
- Screwdrivers: cross-head and slotted
- Craft knife
- Sanding block
- Adhesive spreader/paint brush
- Flat second cut file
- Chisels: 8 mm, 25 mm bevel-edge
- Electric router with straight cutter and 5 mm grooving bit
- Hacksaw
- Marking gauge

PREPARATION

1 Remove skirting boards from the area where the cupboard will be installed (see page 21).

2 On the melamine mark out the dividers and shelves. Then, use a circular saw to cut out the pieces. Remember to cut on the waste side of the marked out lines.

THE DIVIDERS

3 Make a template for the adjustable shelf holes. On a scrap piece of chipboard 100 mm wide and 1 m long, mark a line 50 mm in and parallel to the edge. Square a line across 200 mm from one end. Then mark several more at even intervals (commercial shelving has the holes 32 mm apart, but 50 mm will suit most applications). Drill a 5 mm hole through the board at each point. Keep the drill square as you must finish with evenly spaced holes.

4 Cramp the template onto a divider flush with the edge and top. Use the same 5 mm bit to drill the holes. To prevent drilling right through the divider, wrap a little masking tape around the bit to indicate the depth of the hole. Work from the top of the divider, drilling holes down both edges on the faces required.

5 Mark the centre of the wall and measure to one side half the thickness of the chipboard (8 mm). Draw a vertical line up the wall the full height of the divider (1800 mm).

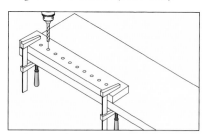

4 Cramp the template onto a divider flush with the edge and top. Use the 5 mm bit to drill the holes.

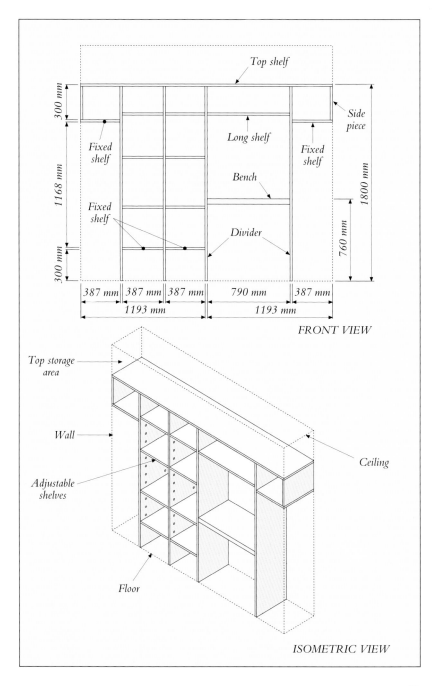

FRONT VIEW

ISOMETRIC VIEW

MELAMINE SHELVING

Edged melamine shelving already cut to 450 mm wide can be purchased from suppliers. It may have a series of holes drilled on one or both faces and these are ideal for adjustable shelf pins. Otherwise, holes can be drilled into the faces of the board where they are needed.

The edges of melamine boards can be very sharp. Wear gloves or remove the sharp edge with abrasive paper.

6 Stand the divider against this line and place the level on the front edge of the divider to check it is vertical. If there are large gaps between the back edge and the wall, mark the back edge and use a sharp hand plane to shape it to match the wall. If possible, hold the divider on edge in a vice or on the floor, taking care not to damage the front edge. Reposition it and check again.

7 Plane the bottom edge to fit against the floor in the same manner.

8 Repeat on the remaining dividers, taking care to maintain the top in the same alignment. To locate their positions, divide the space on one side of the first divider equally by three (387 mm) and then number each divider to avoid mixing them up. Place the fourth divider 790 mm on the other side. (See the diagram on page 57.)

THE SHELVES

9 Cut the four fixed shelves to size (387 mm) with either a hand or circular saw. Straighten the edges with a plane. Use a builders square to help maintain a square edge. If using a circular saw, cramp a straight edge to the board to act as a guide.

10 The two lower fixed shelves are dowelled to the dividers. Measure up 300 mm from the bottom of the dividers and square a line across on both sides of the centre divider and on one side of the other two dividers (make one left-handed and one right-handed).

11 On the shelf, measure 25 mm in from the front and the back edges. Square a pencil line across the face and down the side edges on each. Square another line across the centre of the shelf. These represent the three dowel positions. Set a dowelling jig with an 8 mm guide collar to bore a hole in the centre of the edge. Cramp the jig over the edge with the centring 'V' on the square lines. Use an 8 mm dowelling bit to bore the holes 15 mm deep and place an 8 mm dowel centre in each hole. Lay each divider on a flat surface and align the shelf with the 300 mm set out. Press the shelf down firmly so that the centres mark the divider. Drill each dowel hole in turn on the centre marks 10 mm deep. Use the depth stop from the dowelling jig to prevent you drilling through the divider.

12 Measure down 300 mm from the top of the left-hand divider on the outside face to find the position for the upper fixed shelf. Repeat on the right-hand divider. Follow step 11 to set out and drill the dowel holes on the outside face only of the dividers.

13 Cut two side pieces to be fixed to the wall, with the top edge in line with the level line for the top of the dividers. Drill two holes through each side piece into the wall and fix them in place with 50 mm x 8 gauge countersunk screws.

14 Position each divider and mark the outer edge on the floor. Measure back 30 mm and drill an 8 mm hole in the floor to line up with the centre. Use a dowel centre to mark the bottom of each divider and bore a similar hole. Insert a dowel in each floor hole.

15 Take one upper fixed shelf, place a little PVA adhesive in each dowel hole and insert the dowels. Align the shelf with the dowel holes in the divider and push them together. Slide the shelf and divider into place so that the shelf fits under the side piece screwed to the wall. Drill two 4.5 mm holes through the shelf and fix the shelf to the bottom edge of the side piece with two 50 mm x 8 gauge countersunk screws. Repeat for the other upper fixed shelf. Position the other dividers and fit the lower fixed shelves in place with 8 mm dowels and adhesive.

16 Cut the top shelf to fit between the walls. It will sit on top of the dividers and side pieces. Drill through the shelf into each divider or side piece, ensuring each is vertical and parallel. Fix with 50 mm screws.

THE BENCH

17 Cut the bench as before using the circular saw and straight edge. Straighten it with a hand plane if required. Lay the bench upside down on a flat solid surface. Apply a little PVA adhesive to the front part and position the chipboard reinforcement on the bench so the front edges are in line. Fix with 25 mm nails. Plane flush with a hand plane if required.

18 The front edge and top face of the bench are covered with plastic laminate, which is cut with a craft knife. Measure the size of the bench and mark it on the face of the laminate, adding 20 mm all round. Lay the laminate on a firm, flat surface. Place a straight edge on the set-out line and score a line along the surface several times until a deep

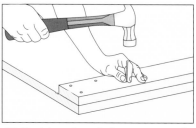

17 Position the reinforcement on the bench so the front edges are in line. Fix with 25 mm nails.

> **HINT**
>
> When using contact adhesive
> make sure you are working in a
> well-ventilated area and don't let
> the adhesive come into contact
> with your skin.

groove is cut into the surface of the laminate. Take care to hold the straight edge firm as any slips of the knife will damage the surface. Repeat this for the edge strip.

19 Hold the bench on edge in a vice and apply one light coat of contact adhesive to the front edge with a paint brush; allow it to dry. Lay the edge strip face down on a scrap piece of timber and apply a coat evenly to the back. Apply a second coat to the edge of the bench at once. Wait until both surfaces are touch dry.

20 Keep the strip in the correct alignment as it will be difficult to remove or alter when it comes into contact with the other surface. Press the strip down well with a cork block wrapped in a clean rag. Be

careful, as the edges of the laminate can be extremely sharp. Use a hand plane and file to ensure the edges are flush. Do not round them over.

21 To laminate the top, lay it on a flat surface. Clean off any dust or excess adhesive. Lay the top laminate face down on the bench and dust off. To spread the contact adhesive out over a large area, use a gloss paint roller or a spreader, or purchase the adhesive in a pressure spray can.

22 Apply adhesive to the laminate and move it out of the way. Do not leave it in direct sunlight or any breeze or the surface will dry too quickly. Apply adhesive to the bench top in the same manner. Keep both surfaces free of dirt and dust, which will be visible under the laminate. When it is touch dry, lay three strips of thin timber (dowels are ideal) on top of the bench. Place the laminate, adhesive side down, on the timber and ensure it will cover the bench all the way around. Start at one end and press the laminate down gently. Work towards the other end, sliding

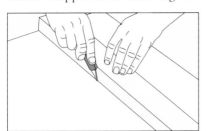

18 Score a line along the surface several times until a deep groove is cut into the surface of the laminate.

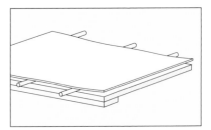

22 Lay three strips of thin timber on top of the bench. Place the laminate, adhesive side down, on the timber.

each strip out as you go. When all the strips have been removed, press the laminate down firmly.

23 Plane and file the edges flush. If desired, you can now file a slight bevel on the front edge to remove any sharp corners.

24 The bench is fixed on a support screwed to the divider. Cut the support to fit between the reinforcement and the back edge of the bench. Drill three 4.5 mm holes through the support each way.

25 Mark the height of the bench (760 mm) on the two dividers and measure down the thickness of the bench (18 mm). Square a line back to the wall. Using 25 mm x 8 gauge screws, fix the support to the dividers with the top in line with this set-out and the end against the wall. Position the bench on the support and screw fix from underneath.

THE BULKHEAD

26 The finished inside face of the bulkhead is in line with the outside

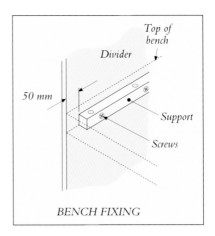

BENCH FIXING

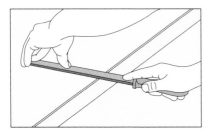

23 If necessary file a slight bevel on the front edge of the bench, removing any sharp corners.

edge of the shelves. Use a spirit level to plumb a line up the wall to mark the position. Cut away any existing cornice to enable the bulkhead frame to fit tightly against the ceiling. Adjust the height of the bulkhead to suit the doors you have purchased and allow for clearances and reveals.

27 Cut the top and bottom plates to fit between the walls (see diagram on page 62). Space the studs 600 mm apart and butt to the plates. For a 200 mm high bulkhead cut them to 130 mm. Nail through the top plate into each stud with 75 x 3.5 mm lost-head nails. Lift the frame into position and nail up through the top plate into the ceiling joists. Fix the two end studs to the wall, by nailing to a wall stud or with hollow wall anchors. Position the bottom plate. Nail up into the bottom of each stud.

28 Cover the bulkhead with plasterboard and fix cornice to match the existing cornices (see page 70).

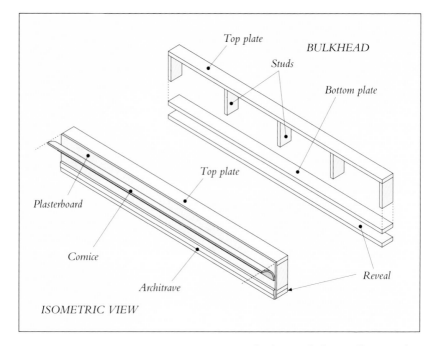

Top plate

BULKHEAD

Studs

Bottom plate

Top plate

Plasterboard

Cornice

Architrave

Reveal

ISOMETRIC VIEW

THE REVEAL LINING

29 Cut the reveal head to fit between the walls. Position it under the bulkhead and check it with a spirit level. Pack the head level and fix it with 65 x 2.75 mm lost-head nails. Keep the edge straight and flush with the outside lining.

30 Cut the two side reveals to length. These fit directly under the head and sit on the floor. Take care to cut the ends square. Hold them against the wall, check with the level that they are vertical and mark a line down the wall with a pencil. Behind each side reveal use four 100 x 50 mm packing pieces 75 mm in from each end and evenly spaced so that the side reveals are vertical and

stand clear of the wall. Fix the packing pieces with 75 mm nails in line with the vertical line.

31 Replace the reveal against the packing pieces and check again that it is vertical. If necessary, small pieces of thin cardboard may be used for minor adjustments. On the reveals, mark the position of the top shelf and square a line across the face. Measure 30 mm down from this and square a second line across for the stopped housing. Square the lines down the back edge and set a marking gauge to mark the depth (6 mm). Reset the marking gauge to match the width of the middle rail (90 mm) and then scribe a line from the back edge.

32 Lay the reveals on a flat surface and use a tenon saw to cut the housing to the gauge line. Remove the waste with a 25 mm bevel-edge chisel. Check the bottom of the joint for level and adjust as required.

33 Reposition one of the reveals and check for vertical on the edge as well as the face. Fix it with two 65 x 2.75 mm lost-head nails into each packer. Prop the second reveal in place and measure the length for the middle rail (from the bottom of each housing). Cut the middle rail to fit between the housings.

34 Fit the middle rail into the fixed reveal. While holding the rail up, slip the second reveal in place with the rail in the housing. Check the reveal for vertical both ways and fix as before. Skew two 65 x 2.75 mm lost-head nails through the top of the middle rail into the reveal.

35 Fix architrave around the reveal both inside and out (see pages 19–21). The outside architrave should match any architraves in the room. Fit the inside one around the shelf. Cut skirting to fit around the floor between the dividers.

THE DOORS

36 If necessary, trim standard doors to fit the openings, making allowance for the sliding track system (see pages 8–10 for trimming a door). Remove all splinters and sharp edges from the doors with abrasive paper.

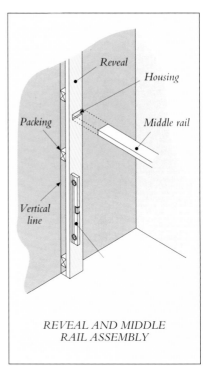

Reveal

Housing

Packing

Middle rail

Vertical line

REVEAL AND MIDDLE RAIL ASSEMBLY

37 Fix the track for the bottom doors, with the track at the top and the guide screwed to the floor.

38 Cut the pelmet and fix it to the face of the middle rail with 50 x 2.5 mm nails so that it covers the track and gap at the top of the door.

39 Fix the track for the top doors, with the track at the bottom and the guide at the top.

TO FINISH

40 Fill any nail holes and lightly sand. Fit handles or flush pulls to the doors and apply the finish of your choice.

Partition wall

Building a simple partition wall can allow you to make the best use of space in your home. A door can be included or the doorway can be left open with the lining and skirting returning around it.

MATERIALS

- Wall plates/studs: 70 x 35 mm pine
- Door frame: 90 x 35 mm pine
- Architrave: 75 x 25 mm
- Wall sheeting: 4.5 mm fibre cement
- 60 mm cornice
- Flush hollow door 2040 x 820 mm
- One pair 75 mm butt hinges
- Privacy latch

- 75 x 3 mm lost-head nails
- 50 x 2.5 mm lost-head nails
- 38 mm plasterboard nails
- Stud adhesive
- Jointing tape and cornice cement
- Plastic drive pins
- Ten 75 mm masonry wall plugs
- Abrasive paper

MEASURING UP

1 Measure the size of the proposed partition at several places from ceiling to floor and wall-to-wall to find out how square the room is. Write down the smallest measurements each way.

2 Check for any pipes or electricity that will be affected by the partition. You may need to move the partition a little or have the pipes or switches relocated by a licensed tradesperson.

3 Mark the position for the inside of the partition on the floor at each end. Stretch a string line between the two points and, with a tape measure, use the 3-4-5 method to check that the line is square to the wall (see page 66). Adjust if necessary. Mark

the set-out positions at both ends and use a chalk line to produce a visible line on the floor. Place a spirit level against the wall on the set-out points and mark a vertical line to the cornice/ceiling. Mark the outside edge of the stud.

MARKING OUT THE PLATES

4 Select the straightest piece of timber and cut a bottom plate to fit between the walls. Make sure that the fit is not too tight.

5 On the bottom plate set out the doorway. Measure in from one end the thickness of the framing timber and square a line across. From this position, mark the width of the framing timber and square another

Passage from the living room to the back garden is much more pleasant now a partition wall has been built to close off the laundry and toilet (see the 'before' photograph on page 70).

TOOLS

- Tape and pencil
- Chalk line
- Square
- Spirit level
- Handsaw
- Chisel: 25 mm
- Electric drill
- Drill bits: 6.5 mm; tungsten-tipped masonry bit
- Hammer
- Screwdriver
- Craft knife or marking knife
- Fibre cement cutter
- Broad knife
- Steel trowel
- Sanding float
- Hand plane
- Keyhole saw or padsaw

line across the face. Then measure the thickness and again square a line right around the bottom plate. These lines represent a collection of studs called a nest of studs. The last stud is the first door stud.

6 To set out the doorway, measure from the first door stud the width of the door, plus twice the frame thickness, plus 20 mm clearance (876 mm for an 820 mm wide door with rebated frames 18 mm thick). Square a line right around the bottom plate. On the face of the plate mark the thickness of a stud (the second door stud).

7 At the opposite end of the plate, set out a nest of studs as before, then divide the distance between this nest and the last door stud by 450 mm spacing and mark the stud locations.

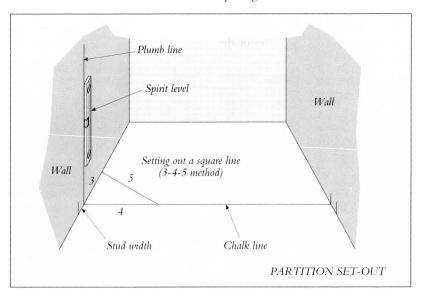

Plumb line

Spirit level

Wall

Setting out a square line (3-4-5 method)

Wall

3

5

4

Stud width

Chalk line

PARTITION SET-OUT

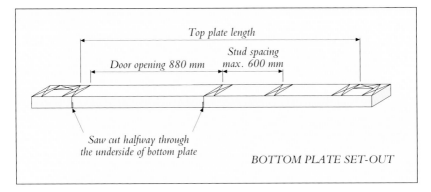

Top plate length

Stud spacing
max. 600 mm

Door opening 880 mm

Saw cut halfway through
the underside of bottom plate

BOTTOM PLATE SET-OUT

The studs should preferably be spaced at 450 mm centre-to-centre. However, they may be at 600 mm centres if required. Mark the location of each stud with a cross.

8 Choosing the next straightest piece, cut the top plate 200 mm shorter than the bottom plate. This represents twice the width and twice the thickness of the framing timber.

9 Lay the top plate beside the bottom plate so that the end of the top plate lines up with the outside edge of the door stud. Transfer the set-out to the top plate using a square. Place a cross where the studs are to be located.

10 If you are using planed (seasoned) timber, the studs can just be butted up against the plates. However, if you are using sawn timber, set out a housing for each stud, working from the outside of the timber to ensure that the bottom of the joints are level. Cut and chisel out each of the housings.

11 Turn the bottom plate upside down and use a handsaw to cut approximately halfway through the thickness on the set-out lines squared around the plate either side of the doorway (see the diagram above).

CONSTRUCTING THE FRAME

12 Cut the studs to length, cutting the end studs 70 mm shorter to clear the cornice when installed (see the diagram on page 68).

13 Construct the frame as near to the job as possible so the partition can be stood in its final position with a minimum amount of lifting. Lay the top and bottom plates on edge. Place the studs between them with any bows on the top. Skew-nail through the outside face of each plate with two 75 x 3 mm lost-head nails into the ends of the studs.

14 Fix blocking pieces (offcuts of stud timber 300 mm long) between the wall stud and intermediate stud at each nest of studs.

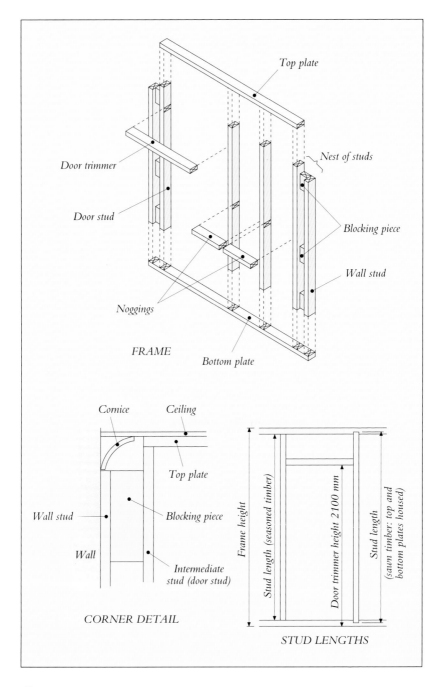

Top plate

Nest of studs

Door trimmer

Door stud

Blocking piece

Wall stud

Noggings

FRAME

Bottom plate

Cornice   Ceiling

Top plate

Wall stud

Blocking piece

Wall

Intermediate
stud (door stud)

CORNER DETAIL

Frame height

Stud length (seasoned timber)

Door trimmer height 2100 mm

Stud length
(sawn timber: top and
bottom plates housed)

STUD LENGTHS

15 Place noggings between all other intermediate studs at a maximum of 1350 mm centres. Skew-nail as before by nailing through the studs into the ends of the noggings. Fix a door trimmer across the doorway at 2100 mm high in the same way.

ERECTING THE FRAME
16 Stand the frame up in the correct location and align it with the vertical lines on the wall and the chalk line on the floor. Add temporary braces as required to hold the frame in position until it is permanently fixed.

17 Place a spirit level on the side of the wall studs and check they are vertical. Adjust as required. Small pieces of thin timber or cardboard may be placed between the wall and studs where they are fixed.

18 Fix the frame to the walls. When fixing to existing timber frames, nail through the partition frame into the existing framework. For masonry walls, use a twist bit and drill three 6.5 mm holes through each wall stud in the top, bottom and centre.

Change the bit for a tungsten-tipped masonry bit and drill through these holes into the wall to a total depth of 75 mm. Place a fastener in each hole and drive the pin in with a hammer. Repeat, fixing the bottom plate to the floor, placing a fastener directly on each side of the door so that they are spaced at 600 mm maximum.

19 Check the frame lines up with the chalk line and is vertical. Nail through the top plate into the ceiling joists with 75 mm nails.

20 Use a handsaw to cut down each side of the door studs to remove that part of the bottom plate. If a large skirting is to be used, nail offcuts of framing timber on top of the bottom plate between the studs.

21 If required, have any services placed in the wall.

ADDING WALL LINING
22 Cut the wall lining to size using a marking knife or soft-sheet cutter for fibre cement. For plasterboard use a straight edge as a guide and a sharp

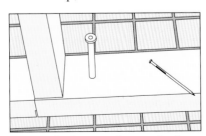

18 Fix the bottom plate to the floor, placing a fastener directly on each side of the door.

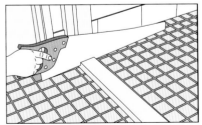

20 Use a handsaw to cut down each side of the door studs to remove that part of the bottom plate.

Before the partition was built the laundry (including the downstairs toilet) was completely open.

craft knife to cut the face first. Turn the board over and then snap the back so that the sheet breaks. Use the knife to cut along the back of the 'v', in order to complete the cut.

23 Apply stud adhesive to the studs and fix the sheets in place with plasterboard nails. Do not use stud adhesive on fibre cement sheets. Nail to all timber every 200 mm and 18 mm from the edges. Hit the nails so that they sit just below the surface of the lining and fill with plaster.

24 Use a broad knife to fill the recess of the joint with a base cement. Before the cement sets, embed perforated paper jointing tape and use a trowel to apply a second layer of base cement slightly wider than the first. When the base coat is thoroughly dry, use a steel trowel to apply a third coat of base cement 200 mm wide. When it is dry apply a finishing cement in the same way but 250 mm wide. Fill any nail holes and sand with 120 grit abrasive paper.

25 Cut the cornice to butt into the existing walls. Batter the joints and back edges with cornice cement. Work quickly as this cement sets rapidly. Push the cornice up tight and evenly over the joints between ceiling and wall. Wipe off the excess with a wet sponge. Don't drown the plasterboard or the paper covering will be damaged. Place a few temporary nails under the cornice to hold it in place until the cement sets.

26 Lightly sand and fill any imperfections or nail holes.

TO FINISH
27 Construct a frame to suit the door, but that is 6 mm wider and 20 mm higher than the door itself. Plane the back edge of the frame to match the overall thickness of the wall. Cut the bottoms level with the tread. Fix them in place and check they aren't twisted. Check the head is level.

28 Use two 75 x 3 mm lost-head nails at three intervals on each frame. You may need packing behind the frame. Fix the architrave and skirting (see pages 19–23) and hang the door (see pages 11–12). Paint as desired.

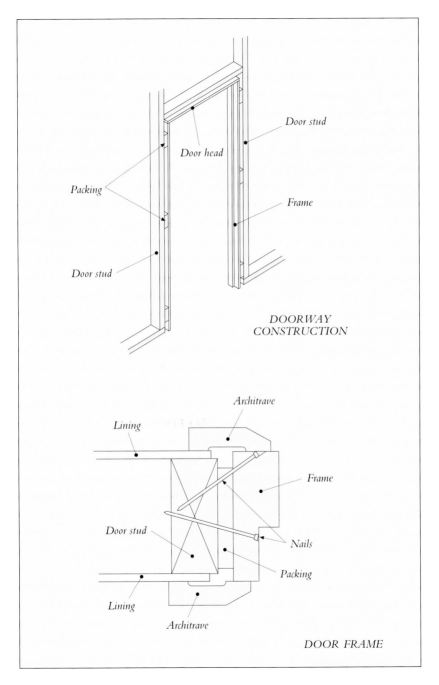

Door stud

Door head

Packing

Frame

Door stud

*DOORWAY
CONSTRUCTION*

Architrave

Lining

Frame

Door stud

Nails

Packing

Lining

Architrave

DOOR FRAME

Index